tree

by Wulf James

July 2020

Anchochaba Publishing © 2020
All rights held by author.

treaty

My land is not barren;
The fruits of my labors flow from my fingertips
To lovers' lips like choke cherry wine--
Bitter, but welcome.
Boundaries blurred by shadows and riverbanks,
You will not find this entity on any colonizers map--
No matter how many ways they try to draw us in.
Our ancestors follow our people,
calling out to fractured souls as we limp
through disconnected fields.
Our colors may have been whitewashed
with centuries of hands pressing the wildflowers
into books written by eyes that never saw the beauty
they wanted tamped down.
Those layers fall away as oil rumbles up from below,
Echoing the calls of our ancestors--
Paint your bodies with the colors around you, children
Wash away the borders colonization talked you into!
We are here--
As long as the grass grows,
And the water runs.

exhibition

if all good stories are told around a campfire,
then let me build one in your bones.
we can use the pit in your stomach
where you tell me you keep
all the dark things and
butterflies pinned to the wall,
an exhibition of all the faded loves
mounted and sealed behind glass,
where they can't hurt you anymore.
i want to see the shadows move across
your lips like herds of wild stallions
impossible to catch, but beautiful.
and as the embers die, and your skeleton
cools in the midnight velvet breeze,
i will bundle up the museum
cataloging each piece with my own descriptions,
showcasing strength and compassion
where you see faults and weakness.
tell me your stories out here under the stars,
let my bones light your bones,
and the rattle of bare souls singe away
the loneliness of the fall.

at Stonewall

all my ancestors danced at stonewall

their skin reflecting the shadows within the fire

one Stonewall was surrounded by windowless walls

the other by forests and smoke

all my ancestors hid from the same man

together they danced, hundreds of miles, years apart

forced on journeys down unforged paths

armed with bricks, with drums, with pride --

all my ancestors danced at Stonewall

bodies turned toward the fire

uplifting their voices to the creator

their cries a rising song to keep our stories, us -- alive.

no treaty, no laws, no promises upheld

all my ancestors still dance at Stonewall

in protest, a promise to ourselves

we are unconquered

we are unconquerable

our drums will beat far longer than our hearts do

and our chepota, our children will dance at Stonewall

two spirits live in me

chikasha soya

and i am proud

Decades

There is a revolution under our skin,
The embers lie banked behind unshuttered eyes,
fighting to break free--
And I intend to fight in it with him.

I long to set fire to each nerve ending,
My breath a blue flame of resolve
Ignited by matchstick fingertips,
Roughened over decades of battles waged
In the name of hieros gamos--
a commitment beyond paper words.

space

somewhere in the darkest corners
of my dilapidated brain there is a space,
the one you carved out when you held up a lopsided smile and a well-used heart,
where the sparkle in your eye
chases demons out, breaks the
stranglehold this build up of anxiety has over me–
and though small it brightens the things around it.
It tastes like you, like lightening, quick and liquid
and warm in my mouth…metallic like blood or
that first rain drop that rolls over your lip
when you tilt your face upward at the first sign of rain.
With the illumination of what has lain dark
for what seems like (and might have been)
centuries, it seems some grotesque and
unwanted artifacts have been unearthed.
Maybe together we can build something strong enough
to contain those relics before the brightness
of this blaze awakens it all fully.

Universe

You are a universe of secrets, little star;

They fill you with mischievous glitter,

the deepest abyss.

I will be your astronaut, braving the unknown,

 exploring open yet unexplored territories, just outside the window

and light years away.

I have nothing to hide, no fear of the dark,

no agenda at all. I don't want to know your secrets,

but I do want to experience them.

You are not simply full of wonder, but are in fact made of it.

I can feel it brush my fingertips as they slip across your skin.

It is an answer to my own hidden universe, held captive behind blue skies.

Others

Some days,

I will unwrap you slowly

Savoring each inch

Of flesh as I reveal it.

Others,

I will be inclined to shred

Anything between your skin

And my mouth,

Especially when the ache I feel

For you makes my teeth chatter

And my bones ache, radiating

Outward into reaching fingertips.

Some days,

I can get by with a hello

Passive communication.

Others,

I want to reach into your skeleton

Sift through the debris between teeth

And spine, excavate unexposed viscera.

On Congress

Dancing skeletons

On creaky wooden floors

Brave enough to come out of the closet

But not all the way out, yet

Go ahead and go to the corner

Shoo, fly on away, you

Spinning yellow prisms

Sir, may I help you

Pay to park

Under an oak tree

Encased in brick and mortar

Twinkle lights struggling to shine

In daylight

Frida Kahlo's likeness

Painted inside discarded bottle caps

skin

I could write poetry on your skin,
But it would hide your beauty- so
Instead I will sit back and watch your
Face light up when you smile, the way
Your quiet laughter tumbles forth like
Wind chimes clinking in a warm
Summer's breeze.
Oh, oh- I just realized!
        You are poetry, just as you are.

pages

I miss your lips, and the way
You pressed them to mine
And held it, as if they're pages
Between which petals lie,
Sunshine scented place markers
For a moment left behind.

I miss the depth, the wondrous cadence
Of your voice, both honeyed and rough
Between warm breaths, against my neck,
In early morning hours spent entangled–
Somehow simultaneously comfortable and free.

Most of all, though, I miss the camaderie,
The blissfully simple act of sharing
Brief moments of little import,
Valued solely by the quality of conversation

butterflies

-for papa

My sides ache
From laughter's spasm
Or perhaps the way you
Nibble at my ribcage
Something about your teeth
Scraping my bones
Must have unleashed
Wondrous things, because
Butterflies once rested just
below them and now, now
They are free

Stars: there's always a fault in them isn't there

I walked outside,

and looked up.

Orion's belt was right above me,

which is where I always put you.

Thank you,

for reminding me

that I'm worth more than that…

that I deserve better than to be second.

Have a nice time lighting up the sky….

and try not to get lost

on the darkness out there.

yosemite

I fell in love with California
Through second hand fairy tales
And the daydream whispers of mountains
Granite monuments to time
Shadows hiding valleys from the sun's warmth
Stealing all the majesty from the sunset skyline
Like a runaway lover with no remorse for heartache
That's the thing about mountains, though
Their stance seems resolute until they're over taken
A river's trickle, a steady wind--
And peaks bow at a rumbling whim
Perhaps I should fall in love with the ocean next

Living with a man just like my father

1.Bile sneaks up my esophagus
Held at bay by gritted teeth
And a stubborn resolution
Not to ever, ever relapse again

2. He says I'm the one who's screaming
His face purple, veins throbbing, almost
Audibly with the raspy rapid inhalations
When the scream goes back inside
To the root of unbridled anger and fear

3. I sit on the floor in the bathroom,
Feet propped casually on the cool painted iron, the thrum of electricity from somewhere else especially loud when everything has gone suddenly silent

4.

5.

6. It took longer than I thought it would for him to notice that I'd locked myself in. Or locked him out, it doesn't really matter which at this point. Handles rattle and door jambs are tapped by shaking doors like a telegraph.

7. I can't breathe this air .stop.
I need a moment of quiet to ease the overwhelming sound of my heart shattering . Full stop.

8. He doesn't stop.

9. I apologize. I promise I will do better next time.

10. There will be a next time. It still won't be my fault. I'll beg anyway. I'll listen to the winds rattle loose every brick holding up this house. There's no Fujita scale to measure the damage from this storm. There is no way to quantify the damage.

bees

you call them thunder thighs
like you don't crave the lightning
between them
maybe curiosity killed the cat
but that's not what i'm terrified of
(it's you)
cats, dogs, birds, bees, who cares
what anyone else is doing
your questions don't give you free entrance
i am not an experiment
i am not something to try
this isn't baskin robbins
i may be delicious
but i am not your flavor of the week

Train wreck

Some places, some times,

Coming out is a train wreck.

Mashed up misgendered carnage

Flung around like a ragdoll.

Deadname shouted like a rebel yell,

As if shouting it over and over

Will make it take over again.

That name, that identity

It is no more me than

Discarded snakeskin

Is still that snake.

You can wave it around all you want,

But you can't make it hiss.

Lay it to rest, with your binary-coded expectations.

I will stand against your self-made war, a self-made man, and I will say my name with the same loving calmness that led you to love me in the first place. It doesn't matter if you say it back.

My voice matters.

My voice is enough.

I am enough.

On Bone

Bits of newsprint,

Snippets of conversations,

Song lyrics--

Pasted to my body like tattoos,

Affixed to the underside of my skin

Next to veins and muscle and tendons...

Words written on bone with indelible ink:

Woman

Sister

Wife

Mother

Bitch

Whore

Dyke

Some people interact with my soul,

And leave pieces of themselves with me--

Poetry and birdsong.

Others rip the ribbons and lace

And leave it tattered, thread-bare

Heart stings plucked and torn like

Ancient guitar strings, too feeble to

Sing a single note without snapping.

And yet I keep gathering odds and ends,

Heated discussions and idle threats,

Curses and whispered 'I love yous,'

And all this adds up

To me

To who I am

And who I will be.

Every word, every look

Every stunning piece of art

Wears off rough edges

Opens new wounds-

Or heals old ones-

And the end result is a

Strong

Proud

Confident

Person

Parent

Writer

Lover

Who wears their life, their soul

Pasted to their body like tattoos,

Affixed to the underside of their skin

Next to veins and muscle and tendons...

Words written on bone with indelible ink.

how to love a person

just press your palm to their palm

warm and full of possibility

skip across their soul like

a flat stone flung from the river's edge

and then sink into them

come to rest amid the silt and debris

wiggle your toes in the particles

of everything they are

you don't have to do anything different

you don't have to try harder

you don't have to re-mold yourself

into something that makes you

somehow less you

and neither do they.

stand beside them

as they meet their true self

let them introduce you to their "me"

as they find it, one bit at a time

or all at once.

gather up their tears, their smiles,

their joys and their discomforts

when they can't carry them anymore

remind them where they're going

go along with them, whenever they ask

witness their struggles and triumphs

open your heart and your arms
press your cheek to their cheek
and love them more when the sun rises
than you did when it set on the day before

i am my own ringmaster

tell me again to put a filter on my mouth
not to think what I think or feel what I feel
I will rail against the walls, beat myself bloody
to be heard, to be seen, to be acknowledged
you cannot put your hand over my mouth
cover my genitalia, check my pockets
and keep one palm on your precious bible at the same time
what's between my legs and my lips is not your concern
so get out of my bedroom, out of my clinic, out of my business
I am not your monkey. This is not your circus. I am my own ringmaster.

peace

i'm sorry i'm sorry i'm sorry i'm sorry i'm sorry
i can't type or say or sing or yell it softly or loudly or on pitch
my lips, my fingertips can't make it true enough for you
i can write poetry on every inch of your skin
but my words are no longer enough to press
the broken pieces close enough together
to form a spinal column with the ability to remain
upright, whole. all the shards and broken bits are
scattered, discarded without a second glance
tossed around like the debris that bounces around
on the floorboard of your car when you slam it into reverse
into my soul, my heart, the last vestiges of strength
the ones i was saving for a rainy day
it's raining baby. it's pouring down all around me,
soaking into the carpets and seeping up through
my toes as i stand here, powerless. no control,
no direction, open palms raised to the sky,
screaming—but the only thing i can hear or see or taste or feel
is this fettered pain that has invaded the borders and settled
in like i am its home and while i am not, it is at peace

Hunger

Songs about rain tend to be sad

But this – rhythmic snick of droplets on unguarded glass --

This doesn't feel sad –

Unheld

Lips cool to the touch,

Cheeks unblushed –

But not sad – contemplative

As the promise of you lingers

Like your scent on my pillows

Hunger like a distant rumble of thunder,

Haphazardly daring me to stop daydreaming

Of the sandpaper bliss of your jawline

And the way you fill my mouth with warmth

Scents – but not the memories – quickly fading tokens of hours upon hours

spent

Entangled

Art

when it comes to the visual arts,
i'm a paint-by-number Picasso -- or
would that be Van Gogh?
I'd have to trace a stick to draw a stick figure,
yet

I feel like I've stared at him long enough
I should be able to draw him from memory
instead, I press these thoughts, these emotions
across the keyboard, instead of into waiting clay
a soft return keeps the thrill of rising gooseflesh
close

I feel like I've held his gaze so intensely
I should be able to fervently describe each sigh

new

Newly printed pages, bound and delivered to waiting hands
No matter what the story, the scent is the same
Newsprint has a musk books don't have -
The nuances of thin paper and warm ink,
Transferred to skin, shared with everything it touches
Some have tried to bottle this essence - new
The result doesn't quite measure up

If it did, I'd beg for a bottle of this
Tentative first kiss, transferred to skin
Marking a path everywhere it touches
Writing its own story on flesh with fingertips
Bound and delivered to waiting lips
The nuances of head tilt and precious tension
Aligning like stars of overlapping constellations
This love has a musk others just don't have
Nobody can bottle this essence
The result could never measure up to you

drops

scents carried on warm summer rain

bring back the tang of your skin between my teeth

the windshield protects my face from the rain drops

the way my rib cage should have protected my heart from you

sunlight streams from behind rain heavy clouds the same way your smile

beamed from eyes shrouded in darkness

pretty words can't hide the scars left behind

but honeyed tongues can trace their paths

carved like raindrops, tears -- sweet healing in their wake

on shirt-sleeves and honesty
-for loksi

I don't think I could survive another decade, another century surrounded by souls with indelible borders, hearts afraid to touch because some of that heart-wrenchingly honest tenderness might bleed over onto someone else's sleeve staining and overflowing, evidence left behind of a love that flows freely like wine, merlot-flavored kisses
I want to hold my shell up to your ear, so you can hear this song, folded up over and around itself, layered like autumn cardigans and bowties. I want to plug my headphones into your heart so that I can listen to it beating from the inside. I want to run my fingertips across your lips and the visceral mess that has been dismantled, taken off display, because museumgoers couldn't handle the reality of the art that is you. You don't have to re-hang the signs and labels, just pull back the white sheets and brush the dust away from the delicate edges. I'll do my own exploring, find my own way home, my own sleeves stained with truth.

Made in the USA
Columbia, SC
27 August 2021